FIRST NATIONS OF NORTH AMERICA

PLAINS INDIANS

W9-AAD-998

ANDREW SANTELLA

HEINEMANN LIBRARY
CHICAGO, ILLINOIS

www.capstonepub.com
Visit our website to find out
more information about
Heinemann-Raintree books.

To order:

☎ Phone 800-747-4992

💻 Visit www.capstonepub.com
to browse our catalog and order online.

© 2012 Heinemann Library
an imprint of Capstone Global Library, LLC
Chicago, Illinois

Original illustrations © Capstone Global Library, Ltd.
Illustrated by Mapping Specialists, Ltd.
Originated by Capstone Global Library, Ltd.

Library of Congress Cataloging-in-Publication Data
Santella, Andrew.
 Plains Indians / Andrew Santella.
  p. cm.—(First nations of North America)
 Includes bibliographical references and index.
 ISBN 978-1-4329-4950-1 (hc)—ISBN 978-1-4329-4961-7
(pb) 1. Indians of North America—Great Plains—Juvenile
literature. 2. Indians of North America—Great Plains—
History—Juvenile literature. I. Title.
 E78.G73S26 2012
 978.004'97—dc22   2010042640

Acknowledgments

The author and publisher are grateful to the following for
permission to reproduce copyright material:

Alamy: Don Smetzer, 23; Bridgeman Art Library: © Brooklyn
Museum of Art /Brooklyn Museum of Art Collection,
cover, Brooklyn Museum of Art, New York, USA Museum
Expedition 1911, Museum Collection Fund, 32, Peter Newark
Western Americana, 26, Private Collection, 38, Private
Collection/Photo © Ken Welsh, 18; Getty Images: Henry
Guttmann, 22, Historical Picture Archive, 27, Michael Ledger,
12, MPI, 30, 31, 36, 39; GRANGER: GRANGER, 24, 37;
Library of Congress: Prints and Photographs Division, 4, 10,
13, 17, 25, 29, 34; Nativestock: Marilyn Angel Wynn, 15, 16, 19,
20, 33, 35; Reuters: Staff, 5; Shutterstock: Jim Parkin, 14, John
McLaird, 9, Rusty Dodson, 8, samotrebizan, 21; SuperStock:
akg-images, 28, Prisma, 40

We would like to thank Zdenek Salzmann, Ph.D., for his
invaluable help in the preparation of this book.

Printed and bound in the USA. 5060

Contents

Some words are shown in bold **like this**. You can find out what they mean by looking in the glossary.

Who Were the First People in North America?

It sounded like an earthquake. A herd of bison charged across a grassy **plain**, their hooves rumbling. Hunters rode on horses at the edge of the herd. Skilled riders, they used only their knees to guide their horses. Each hunter was trying to get close enough to one of the bison to aim a killing blow at the animal's heart. The hunters knew that their families depended on the bison for food and clothing.

These hunters were the early people of the Great Plains of North America. For many of the native peoples who lived on the Great Plains, hunting bison was a way of life. Today, bison no longer roam freely across the Great Plains. But the Plains Indians proudly keep alive many of their customs and traditions.

▲ The bison hunt was at the center of Plains Indian life.

◄ Carl Venne (1946-2009) was a leader of the Crow **Nation** of Montana. He worked to create opportunities for his people.

American Indian or Native American?

Sometimes the native peoples of North America are referred to as American Indians. Sometimes they are called Native Americans. So which is correct? When Italian explorer Christopher Columbus came to the Americas in 1492, he used the names "indios" or "Indians" to describe the native people. This was because he mistakenly believed he was in the Indies—an old term for Asia. "Native American" came into use in the 1960s, as an alternative to "Indian."

Today, many of these descendants of the first people to live in North America would say that either term is acceptable. Better still, most would prefer to be identified by their unique group, called a nation or **tribe**—for example, "I'm a Cheyenne."

The first North Americans

People have lived in what is now the United States for more than 12,000 years. Scientists believe people **migrated** there by walking across a land bridge that once linked North America to Asia. Then, over many years, these people spread out across North and South America.

These early peoples survived by hunting large animals and gathering wild plants. Most of what we know about these early peoples comes from the objects they left behind. **Archaeologists** have discovered stone tools and animal bones that suggest people were living on the Great Plains at least 10,000 years ago.

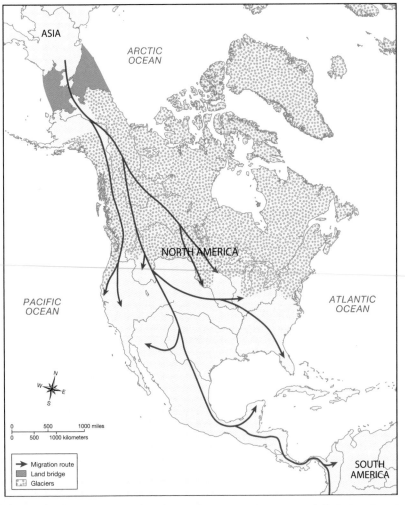

◄ This map shows some routes early peoples took as they spread across North America.

◄ This map shows the 10 American Indian culture areas of North America.

Culture areas

People who study American Indians divide North America into 10 **culture areas**. Each culture area has its own distinctive **geography**, **climate**, and ways of life. Before European explorers arrived, several million American Indians thrived across North America. They spoke many languages and had unique customs, beliefs, and legends. Peoples who lived in the same culture area often had similar lifestyles.

What Are the Great Plains?

The Great **Plains** area is an immense grassland in the middle of North America. It stretches from the Mississippi River to the Rocky Mountains, and from Canada's Saskatchewan River to Texas. It covers parts of 14 U.S. states and three Canadian **provinces**.

The region's tall grasses bend in the strong winds that blow across the landscape. There are some wooded areas, especially along rivers and creeks, where willow and cottonwood trees grow. But none of the large forests found in other parts of North America exist in the Great Plains. While much of the region is flat, there are a few hilly areas. These include the Ozark Mountains of Missouri and Arkansas and the Black Hills of South Dakota.

▲ Tall grasses bend in the strong winds that blow across the Great Plains.

Climate

On the Great Plains, extreme weather is common. Winters can be bitterly cold, with frequent snowy blizzards. Summers bring scorching heat and high winds. On the western Great Plains, only between 10 and 20 inches (25 to 50 centimeters) of rain falls each year. Short, tough grasses thrive in this dry **climate**. Further east, rainfall increases to 20 to 40 inches (50 to 100 centimeters) each year. This extra moisture helps grasses of the **prairies** near the Mississippi River grow very tall. Grasses there can grow as high as 12 feet (3.7 meters) tall.

▲ Winter brings extreme cold and snow to the Great Plains.

Who Are the Indians of the Great Plains?

On the dry western Great **Plains**, early Indians lived mainly by hunting bison. Instead of living in permanent villages, they often moved from place to place, following bison herds and gathering wild plants. They became expert hunters and came to depend on the bison for most of their needs.

Indian groups of the Great Plains

Some of the Plains Indians groups, or **tribes**, had once been farmers in the woodlands of Minnesota, Wisconsin, and Iowa. These people include the Cheyenne, Arapaho, and Sioux. Around 1400 they moved to the Great Plains and adopted a **nomadic** lifestyle. Plains peoples roamed widely, but most tribes could usually be found in particular areas. For example, the Arapaho hunted mainly in Colorado, and the Cheyenne hunted mainly in Wyoming.

▲ Early Plains Indians were often on the move.

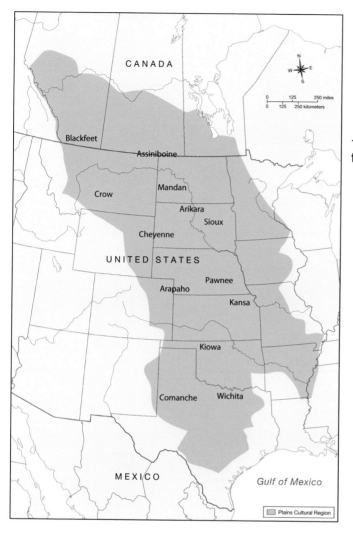

◄ This map shows some of the traditional **tribal** homelands of the Great Plains.

The Sioux were one of the largest Plains tribes and were made up of several different groups. The Teton Sioux (or Dakota) and the Yankton Sioux (or Nakota) occupied the Black Hills of South Dakota and lands to the west.

The Blackfeet people and the Assiniboine people could be found in northern Montana, along the present-day border between the U. S. and Canada.

The Crow people lived to the south along the Yellowstone River.

The area that is now Texas and Oklahoma was home to the Kiowa and Comanche. Both tribes were famous for their skilled horsemen. In fact, the Comanche were among the first Indians to acquire horses from the herds that Spanish explorers brought to North America in the 1600s (see page 17).

Farmer-hunters of the Great Plains

On the eastern Great Plains, more plentiful rainfall created conditions favorable to farming. Tribes in these areas raised crops such as corn, beans, and squash. Like tribes to the west, they also hunted buffalo. But they did not share the nomadic lifestyle of the western Plains Indians. Because their farms provided much of what they needed to survive, they were able to live in villages for most of the year.

The Wichita people lived along the Arkansas River. In the 1500s, they were among the first Plains Indians to meet Europeans.

Further north were the Kansa people, who **migrated** to present-day Kansas from their original home east of the Mississippi River.

▲The Mandan people were among the largest of the Plains farming tribes.

The Pawnee were one of the largest farming tribes. They lived along Nebraska's Platte River.

The Mandan built their villages on high **bluffs** along the Missouri River in North Dakota.

How the Mandan came to be

Most Indian tribes tell stories of how their people came to be. These stories, called origin tales, are passed down from generation to generation. According to their stories, the Mandan people emerged from the Earth, just as their crops do. They say that long ago, the Mandan lived underground. Some brave Mandan climbed a huge vine to reach the earth above them. Seeing how beautiful the land was, they convinced the rest of their people to join them on the surface.

▲ This grass lodge belonged to the Pawnee.

What Animals Did Early Plains Indians Need?

Plains Indians depended on several different kinds of animals to provide many of their daily needs. The bison was at the center of life for the early Plains Indians. The bison is the largest land animal to roam North America in modern times. Even though an adult weighs as much as about 1 ton (1 tonne), or over 2,000 pounds (900 kilograms), bison can still run at speeds of around 30 miles (48 kilometers) per hour. For thousands of years, bison roamed the Great Plains in huge herds.

▲ Bison roamed the Great Plains in enormous herds.

These enormous animals provided most of what Plains peoples needed to live. Plains Indians were experts at hunting bison and at making use of every part of the animal. The clothes they wore and the cone-shaped tents they lived in, called **tipis**, were made from bison **hides**. They sharpened the bones of bison and carved them into tools. They used the horns of bison to make spoons, cups, rattles, and toys. They braided shaggy bison hair into rope.

Of course, bison were an important source of food, too. After men hunted the animals (see pages 18 and 19), women cut up the bison meat. They preserved some of it for later by cutting it into long strips and hanging it to dry on racks in the hot Sun. Once meat was dried this way, it could be stored for long periods without spoiling.

The bison was like a walking store, providing food, clothing, tools, and more. Even bison waste was put to use. Plains Indians used it as fuel for their campfires.

▲ Plains women dried bison meat in the Sun to preserve it for later use. This method is still used to dry meat today.

▲ Before they acquired horses, Plains Indians depended on dogs to help them move heavy loads.

Transportation

Before they acquired horses, early Plains Indians traveled on foot. They relied on dogs to carry heavy loads as they followed bison herds across the plains. They loaded their supplies and belongings onto a kind of sled called a **travois** (pronounced "tra-VOY"). A travois was made of two poles tied together in a V shape, with strips of rawhide stretched across the V. The travois was attached to the shoulders of a dog, which dragged the load behind itself (see photo above).

Horses

The first modern horses were brought to North America by Spanish explorers in the 1600s. Small, early horses had once lived in North America millions of years ago, but they had died out by about 9,000 BCE. Plains Indians began to acquire horses through trading with other **tribes** or by raiding other tribes. By the late 1700s, horses were common among Plains Indians.

Horses changed the way Plains Indians lived. With horses, Plains Indians could travel farther and faster than ever before. It made their **nomadic** lifestyle easier, allowing them to move their camps from place to place as they followed the bison. Plains Indians also found that they could track and hunt bison more effectively on horseback. Tribes such as the Crow gave up their farming lifestyle to become nomadic hunters. Horses also made them more effective warriors, able to attack their enemies quickly and suddenly.

◄ Plains Indians became skilled riders.

Hunting

Hunting was one of the most important parts of the Plains Indian **culture**. Plains Indians hunted many animals, but none was more important to them than the bison. The nomadic tribes moved from place to place to stay close to the wandering bison. Farming tribes of the **prairies** left their villages each summer to take part in annual hunts.

Hunting was a community activity for the peoples of the Great Plains. Men, women, and children worked together to make a successful hunt. The bravest and most skillful hunters and warriors sometimes acted as the hunt "police." Their job was to organize the other hunters so that they worked as a team.

▲ Plains hunters carefully made their own weapons.

▲ Women **tanned** bison hides to make clothes and other objects.

Plains Indians developed clever techniques for hunting bison. Hunters on foot might sneak up on a herd by covering themselves in wolf skins. This way, they could get close to the animals without alarming them. Another strategy was to start grass fires that would frighten the bison into **stampeding** to their deaths off tall cliffs. After Plains Indians acquired horses, they became skillful riders who could hunt while moving at high speeds.

When the hunt was over and the bison were killed, there was still much work to do. Women worked to preserve the meat for future use (see page 15). They also worked at tanning the bison hide, turning it into leather that could be used for robes and bedding.

What Did Early Plains Indians Farm?

Farming was the main source of food and wealth for those early **Plains** Indians that lived in villages. Farming **tribes** lived on very **fertile** land along the major rivers of the Great Plains. With plentiful rain and good growing conditions, they could grow more corn and other crops than they needed. Extra crops could be traded with other tribes for metal tools, cloth, bison **hides**, and other valuable goods.

Farming was mainly the work of women. They planted the fields, tended them, and harvested the crops. Their tools were made from things found in the natural world around them. They used animal bones, horns, and antlers to make hoes and rakes. Women also made clay pots for storing food.

▶ Plains Indians used bones from bison and other animals to make farming tools.

The Three Sisters

Corn, or *maize*, as American Indians called it, was the most important crop for most tribes. It grew well in many areas, was easily stored, and could be prepared in a variety of ways. It could be used in soups and stews, or it could be dried and pounded into cornmeal. Women used wooden tools called **pestles** to grind dried corn into meal.

Farming tribes almost always planted corn alongside squash and beans. Corn stalks provided a pole for bean vines to climb. The leaves of the squash plants helped keep the soil moist. Because the three crops worked so well together, they were often called "the Three Sisters." Farming tribes also grew pumpkins, sunflowers, and tobacco.

► Corn was a basic crop for Plains farming tribes.

What Were Early Plains Indian Communities Like?

The **nomadic** hunters of the early Great **Plains** lived in **tipis**. Tipis were made of bison **hides** sewn together. The hides covered a frame of wooden poles that formed a cone shape. Inside the tipi was a fire pit lined with rocks. Beds made of bison hides were arranged around the fire. People often decorated tipi covers with painted figures that represented the family or showed the great deeds of the hunter or warrior who lived inside.

As people moved across the Great Plains, they carried their tipis with them. Tipis could be quickly taken apart and put back together with each move to a new camp.

◄ Large tipis might be made of as many as 18 bison hides.

Houses of farming peoples

Since the farming **tribes** of the **prairie** did not move around as much as the nomadic hunters, they built more permanent homes. The Wichita and Caddo people built grass houses by covering a circular framework of wooden poles with thick bundles of grass called **thatch**.

Other farming tribes lived in earth lodges with dome-like roofs. These lodges were made of heavy timber posts covered by willow branches and layers of sod (the surface layer of the ground) and earth. People entered their lodge through a covered tunnel. This led to a roomy interior that could hold a number of families or related persons. Like the hunting tribes, farming peoples also used tipis, but only for their yearly hunting trips onto the Great Plains.

▲ Wood could be hard to find on the Great Plains, so people used sod and earth to build houses.

Villages

The farming tribes of the prairies lived in permanent villages. Some of the larger tribes, such as the Pawnee of Nebraska, were made up of 10 or more villages. Farming tribes usually settled near large rivers or streams, which provided water to maintain their farms.

These tribes arranged their lodges close to each other at the center of the village. Farm fields were located at the edge of the village, surrounding their lodges. Villages offered protection from enemy raiders.

The Mandan and Arikara people established their villages on **bluffs** high above the Missouri River. This allowed them to spot any approaching enemies. The Mandans also surrounded their villages with high fences with pointed stakes, called **palisades**, for added security. Other tribes built large mounds of packed earth called **ramparts** to protect their villages.

▲ This painting by George Catlin shows an Arikara village on the Grand River in South Dakota.

▲ Tipis were suited to the nomadic lives of Plains hunters.

Some villages became major trading centers, where tribes from around the Great Plains gathered. They exchanged valuable goods like dried corn, buffalo hides, and beaver furs.

Bands

The nomadic tribes did not settle in permanent villages. In the winter, they split into small **bands**, or groups, to hunt bison and small **game**. In the spring and summer, as the bison gathered in large herds, the Indians came together as tribes. These summer gatherings gave them the chance to meet as a tribe and discuss the future of their people. Some camps might include 1,000 people, with tipis set up in a huge circle.

Clans

In an early Plains Indian family, everyone worked together to support each other. Aunts, uncles, and grandparents all helped parents educate and raise the children.

Family members were also part of larger units called **clans**. A clan is a group of people who share a common **ancestor**, or family member from the distant past. In some tribes, membership in a clan was passed on from mothers to their children. In others, clan membership was passed on from fathers to their children.

▶ **Cradleboards** allowed Plains Indian women to keep their infants with them while they worked.

26

Roles for men and women

Men and women each had their own roles to play in daily life. For men, life revolved around hunting and warfare. They trained and tended horses, and they made weapons such as bows, arrows, and **lances**. They also were leaders, making decisions about where their people should hunt and whether they should start a war.

Women tended farm fields and homes. They put up and took down tipis. They made clothing, hauled firewood, and prepared meals. They cared for children and carried infants on their back in baby carriers called cradleboards as they worked.

A DAY IN THE LIFE OF AN EARLY PLAINS INDIAN CHILD

On a typical day in an early Plains Indian village, children might listen to storytellers tell about the history of their people. Boys might prepare to become warriors and hunters by learning to ride horses and shoot bows and arrows at targets. Girls would probably learn the skills of cooking, sewing, and other crafts as they helped their mothers.

▲ Family was very important to early, as well as modern, American Indians. Adults taught children the skills they would need to survive.

27

How Were Early Plains Indian Tribes Organized?

Early **Plains** Indian **tribes** were made up of **bands** or villages that were led by **chiefs**. Leaders became chiefs by demonstrating bravery in warfare or great skill in hunting. Chiefs were highly respected, but they did not give orders to the rest of the people. Instead, they tried to guide their people and offer wise advice.

Chiefs led with the help of councils made up of other respected men. The Cheyenne were led by a council of 44 chiefs representing the tribe's various bands. When the bands gathered each summer, their leaders met to discuss issues facing their people. The Cheyenne people still maintain a council of 44 people today.

▶ This painting from 1832 shows a Blackfeet chief named Buffalo Bull's Back Fat.

◄ During council meetings, people smoked pipes like the one this Crow man is holding.

Plains Indians made important decisions only after much discussion and after everyone had the chance to express an opinion. Comanche leaders would gather in a circle to discuss concerns, with each person taking a turn speaking.

LANGUAGE

Sign language

Because they traveled so widely, the Plains Indians often encountered people of other tribes. In many cases, tribes spoke languages so different from each other that communication would be impossible. So Plains Indians developed a sign language system that all could use and understand. They used hand and arm **gestures** to communicate ideas. Their "hand talk" was especially useful when people of many different tribes gathered to trade.

War

Early Plains Indians took great pride in showing their bravery in battle. A warrior who was successful in battle became a hero to his people. Groups of warriors raided other tribes to capture horses, gain wealth, and win glory. One of the greatest feats a warrior could achieve was to "count coup." This meant striking an enemy with a weapon or bare hands and escaping unharmed. Only a warrior who had the courage to get close enough to his enemy to touch him could claim to have counted coup.

▲ This painting from the 1800s shows Plains warriors battling on horseback.

Special societies

Warriors who won the respect of their people became members of special societies reserved for the bravest and strongest. The Cheyenne had a society of warriors called Dog Soldiers who led them in battle and on hunts. Some tribes had as many as eight or ten such societies. These societies competed against each other in games at **tribal** gatherings.

Members of honor societies went to great lengths to show their courage. Among the Kiowa, warriors sometimes staked their sash into the ground during a battle. This was a signal that the warrior would remain there and keep fighting until death, if necessary. When a great warrior reached old age, he became a leader among his people. Among the Lakota Sioux, elderly warriors joined "headman" societies and were looked to for guidance and wisdom.

▶ This painting from the 1830s shows a Mandan chief named Four Bears. The eagle feathers in his headdress were earned by performing great deeds.

What Objects Did Early Plains Indians Create?

The early **Plains** Indians were skilled at making everyday items that suited their **nomadic** way of life. They made rawhide pouches called **parfleches**. Plains Indians used these to carry the food they would need on a long journey. Parfleches were strong, light, and easy to carry. Plains women decorated them with bright colors and geometric designs. Modern Plains Indians continue to make parfleches today.

Decorative arts

Plains women decorated their clothing with porcupine quills. They colored the quills using dyes made from plants. They then arranged the quills to create brightly colored patterns. Warriors wore headdresses made of bison horns or eagle feathers. The eagle feathers were earned by performing heroic deeds or showing bravery (see the painting on page 31).

▲ Plains Indians women decorated these containers called parfleches.

Winter counts

Plains Indians pass their history on from generation to generation by telling stories of great events in their **tribe's** past. To keep a record of these events, they use something called a "winter count." For early Plains Indians, a winter count was a series of pictures painted on a bison **hide**. Each picture represented the most important event from a year in the tribe's history. The scenes were painted in a spiral pattern, with the earliest event in the center and the most recent on the edge.

Looking at the winter count would allow storytellers to remember and pass the people's history on to younger generations. When buffalo became harder to find, Plains Indians began keeping winter counts on paper or other fabric.

▲ A winter count is a painted record of a people's past.

What Did Early Plains Indians Believe?

For the early peoples of the Great **Plains**, religion was a part of everyday life. They believed that everything in the natural world around them was made by a great creator spirit. Because they believed spirits lived in the animals, plants, earth, and even the wind and rain, they were taught to treat nature with great respect. They gave thanks to these spirits and asked for their help.

▲ This photograph from the early 1900s shows participants prepared for a Sun Dance.

▲ Plains Indians sought guidance from spirits by going on **vision quests**. This man is reenacting a Sioux medicine man on a vision quest.

Vision quests

Beginning when they were teenagers, early Plains Indians went on vision quests. A person went off alone for days at a time to **fast** and pray. The goal was to experience a vision that would allow the person to communicate with a spirit. The spirit would guide him for the rest of his life.

Sun Dance

Almost all Plains **tribes** practice the Sun Dance to give thanks to the spirits and celebrate the work of the great creator. Different tribes practice different versions of the dance. Usually a yearly event, it includes community dancing, chanting, and praying. By offering their **sacred** dances and prayers, they hope for continued strength and success. Some Plains Indians practice the Sun Dance today, and the **ceremony** continues to develop over time.

How Did Contact with Non-Indians Affect Plains Indians?

The Spanish explorer Francisco Vázquez de Coronado came to the **plains** of Kansas in 1541. He reported meeting Indians in "skin tents" who hunted "wild cows." He was the first European to meet Plains Indians and to see their **tipis** and the bison they hunted.

Spanish, French, and later U.S. traders came to the Great Plains in search of valuable bison **hides**. The Indians acquired guns from these traders. This made them more effective hunters and more fearsome warriors.

▲ Explorer Francisco Vásquez de Coronado led Spanish soldiers across the southern Great Plains.

▲ Non-Indian hunters killed bison for their hides.

Tragically, white traders also brought with them smallpox and other diseases. This took a terrible toll on Plains Indians. Thousand of Plains Indians died of such diseases, and some entire **tribes** were wiped out.

Settlers move west

As the United States expanded westward in the late 1800s, non-Indian settlers began to move across the Great Plains. Trails and railroads began to stretch across the Great Plains all the way to California. At the same time, non-Indian hunters trying to sell bison hides for profit **slaughtered** the animals by the hundreds and thousands. Bison nearly died out in the 1800s.

Farmers and ranchers looking for land set their sights on the Great Plains. Even though Indians considered the Great Plains their home, settlers saw the land as open country that they could simply take.

War for the Great Plains

In the mid-1800s, the U.S. government tried to force Plains Indians to move to **reservations**. Reservations were public lands set aside as homelands for Indians. On reservations, the Plains Indians would have to give up many of their traditional ways of life and depend on the government for support.

Plains Indians fought back. In 1876 thousands of Lakota Sioux and Cheyenne warriors wiped out a force of U.S. soldiers led by General George Custer, near the Little Bighorn River in Montana. Custer's defeat only made the United States more determined to conquer the Plains Indians.

▲ This painting shows the last moments of the Battle of Little Bighorn.

▲ The Ghost Dance, shown here in a newspaper from 1891, became popular among Indians on reservations in the late 1800s.

Reservations

The U.S. Army began to capture **bands** of Plains Indians. By the 1880s, the last of the Plains Indians had been confined to reservations. The U.S. government promised Indians that they would be taken care of on the reservations. But too often Plains Indians found only poverty and sickness.

Some turned to a new movement called the Ghost Dance religion, which taught that a **sacred** dance would restore the bison and force non-Indian settlers to leave. Some Lakota Sioux participating in a Ghost Dance clashed with U.S. soldiers at Wounded Knee, South Dakota, in 1890. Over 150 Lakota were killed, and the Ghost Dance movement faded. The wars for the Great Plains were over.

What Is Modern Life Like for Plains Indians?

At the start of the 1900s, life on the **reservations** was harsh. People on reservations were very poor and had poor-quality health care.

▲ At gatherings like the one at the Crow Fair in Montana, native peoples of the **prairie** celebrate their traditions.

Reforms brought some improvement. First, in 1924, the U.S. Congress passed the Indian Citizenship Act. This made all Indians citizens of the United States. The Indian Reorganization Act of 1934 tried to give Indians more control over their lives and allow them to practice traditional **ceremonies**. But some **Plains** reservations remained among the poorest places in the country.

In 1968 Plains Indians played a leading part in forming the American Indian Movement (AIM). This group fights for Indians' rights. In 1973 members of the AIM took over the village of Wounded Knee for 71 days. Their actions focused attention on the problems faced by American Indians.

Plains Indians today

Today, Plains Indians live not only on reservations, but also in cities, suburbs, and small towns all across the United States and throughout the world. At **tribal** colleges, people can prepare for employment and learn about traditional ways. More and more Plains Indians are taking an interest in the languages and traditions of their people. At gatherings they dress in colorful costumes and proudly perform traditional dances. By remembering their proud history, they prepare for successful futures.

BIOGRAPHY

Billy Mills

Billy Mills (born 1938) is an Oglala Lakota (Sioux) who was raised on the Pine Ridge Indian Reservation in South Dakota. In 1964 he won the gold medal in the 10,000-meter race in the Olympics in Tokyo, Japan. He later helped found Running Strong for American Indian Youth, a group that helps young American Indians in need.

Timeline

about 10,000 BCE   People cross the Bering Land Bridge into North America.

about 500 CE   Native peoples of the Great **Plains** begin farming.

1541   Spaniard Francisco Vázquez de Coronado explores the southern Great Plains.

about 1700   Plains **tribes** begin to acquire horses.

1841   Settlers bound for Oregon begin crossing the Great Plains on the Oregon Trail.

1864   Colorado volunteers attacked a Cheyenne village in the Sand Creek Massacre, killing hundreds of men, women and children.

1869   Railroads stretch across the Great Plains to span the entire continent.

1876   U.S. General George Custer and the 7th Cavalry are defeated by the Lakota Sioux and Cheyenne at Little Bighorn.

late 1800s   Bison nearly die out because of too much hunting.

1890   Sioux Ghost Dancers are killed by the U.S. Army at Wounded Knee, South Dakota.

1924   The Indian Citizenship Act makes all Indians full citizens of the United States.

1934   The Indian Reorganization Act grants Indians more power to govern themselves.

1960   Ben Reifel elected to House of Representatives from South Dakota, the first Sioux elected to Congress.

1964   Billy Mills wins a gold medal at the Olympics in Tokyo.

1968   The American Indian Movement is founded.

1973   American Indians occupy the village of Wounded Knee for 71 days.

1990   Congress passes the Native American Languages Act, "to preserve, protect, and promote the rights and freedoms of all Native Americans to use, practice, and develop Native American languages."

1990   U.S. Congress passes act declaring November American Indian Heritage Month.

1992   Ben Nighthorse Campbell of the Northern Cheyenne elected to United States Senate from Colorado.

2004   The National Museum of the American Indian is established on the National Mall in Washington, D.C.

Glossary

ancestor family member from the distant past

archaeologist scientist who studies items left behind by ancient people to learn about the past

band small, loosely organized division of a tribe

bluff high, steep bank

ceremony religious event or observance

chief leader of a tribe or group of people

clan group of people who share a common ancestor

climate typical weather conditions of a place or region

cradleboard wooden frame used to carry a baby

culture shared ways of life and beliefs of a group of people

culture area region of North America in which Indians traditionally had a similar way of life

fast to go without eating

fertile able to produce plentiful crops

game wild animals hunted for food

geography science that deals with the location of things on Earth

gesture body movement that expresses a feeling or idea

hide skin of an animal

lance weapon made of a long shaft with a sharp point, used on horseback

migrate move from one place to another

nation community of people with its own organization or government

nomadic moving from place to place without a fixed home

palisade high fence of pointed stakes set up to defend a place

parfleche small container used by American Indians for carrying dried food while traveling

pestle club-shaped tool used for pounding or grinding things

plain broad area of level country

prairie large area of flat grassland

province division of a country with its own government

rampart thick wall used to protect a fort or settlement

reservation area of land in the United States put aside for the use of American Indians

sacred holy or having to do with religious belief

slaughter kill a large number of animals

stampede wild rush of many frightened animals

tan turn animal hides into leather

thatch thick bundle of grass, roots, and other natural material

tipi portable, tent-like dwelling made with wooden poles and animal skins

travois sled made of poles used by American Indians to transport their belongings

tribal belonging to a tribe or group of people

tribe group of American Indians who share a culture

vision quest process involving fasting and praying by which American Indians seek guidance from spirits

Find Out More

Books

Hossell, Karen. *Francisco Coronado*. Chicago: Heinemann Library, 2003.

King, David C. *First People: An Illustrated History of American Indians*. New York: Dorling Kindersley, 2008.

National Museum of the American Indian. *Do All Indians Live in Tipis?* New York: HarperCollins, 2007.

Websites

Blackfeet Nation
www.blackfeetnation.com
Learn more about the Blackfeet nation at the group's official website.

Comanche Nation of Oklahoma
www.comanchenation.com
Learn more about the Comanche nation at the group's official website.

Northern Cheyenne Tribe
www.cheyennenation.com
Learn more about the Northern Cheyenne at the group's official website.

PBS's "We Shall Remain"
www.pbs.org/wgbh/amex/weshallremain/
This is a companion site to the PBS television series, "We Shall Remain;" a series about the role of American Indians in U.S. history.

Places to visit

Little Bighorn Battlefield National Monument
Crow Agency, MT
www.nps.gov/libi/

Museum of the Plains Indian
Browning, MT
www.doi.gov/iacb/museums/museum_plains.html

Buffalo Bill Historical Center
720 Sheridan Ave.
Cody, WY
www.bbhc.org

Eiteljorg Museum of American Indians and Western Art
500 West Washington St.
Indianapolis, IN
www.eiteljorg.org

National Museum of the American Indian
Fourth Street and Independence Avenue, SW
Washington, D.C.
www.nmai.si.edu

Further research

What parts of the Plains lifestyle did you find the most interesting? How does life for native peoples in the Plains compare to the way native peoples live today in other regions? How did the peoples who first lived in your area contribute to life today? To learn more about the Plains or other culture areas, visit one of the suggested places on these pages or head to your local library for more information.

Index